maybe i'm bad

maybe i'm bad

poems, thoughts, and illustrations

by amie james

for m.

contents

uppers 13

downers 49

placebo 85

i am no poet

nor artist

so if you think that maybe i'm bad

fair enough

x

uppers

i am
better during the night
when the sun has gone

i am away from
judgement

i am
calm

x

maybe i'm bad

they told me
people are always good at something

i think then i am good at failing
or maybe at trying

can one exist without the other?
for all flowers grow from soiled ground

x

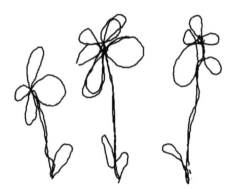

amie james

i
wanna go
for a drive on the highway
at midnight
with no one around
but the trees that stand past the lines

i wanna drive
with the windows down and scream

scream all those worries and frustrations

let the trees dampen the sounds
so no one beyond this passing point can hear

i will go for a drive on the highway at midnight
to let
what is
wild

out

x

maybe i'm bad

i fight tooth and nail
to live another
unextraordinary day
filled with
extraordinary people

x

with someone close

touch
slow

their fingers with yours
watch
as they meet

when held with
an inch void between

watch
the electrical exchange
fly

our blind eyes
cannot see it

only feel it
close sight
and
sense our light
strike soul

x

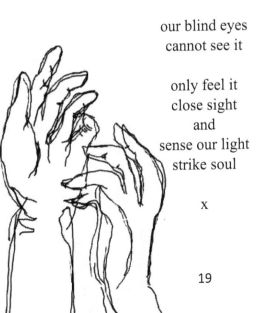

maybe i'm bad

do you ever get that urge
to run a red light

not because you were in a hurry
or you were cutting that amber

but because you were curious
if you could get away with it

the thrill of getting away with
something you shouldn't have

steal a bottle of nail polish

cheat on a pop quiz

dash on a classic dine

to crave and concede
to that velvet voice
of your fiend conscious

x

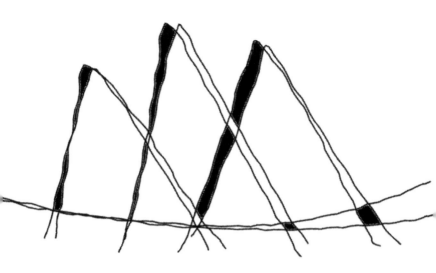

we siblings
the three peaks
of greatest alps

      with own heights
      each supported
      through joint rock

            to stand strong
            together through
            any coming force

x

maybe i'm bad

i slept with an older man
to rattle my cage

exuding experience
i thought him up
to the challenge

he shook the bars a little
but i walked out the same

x

hey

i can taste your saltiness from here

so please step back

i'm trying to cut back on my sodium

x

maybe i'm bad

as an
ocean cliffside
my pride erodes with
each crushing wave
but if this face should crumble
let rock turn dust nurtured by sea
maybe then will my sage finally grow

x

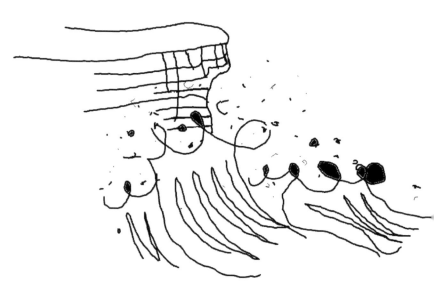

i'm going on a date tonight
he's nice
really nice

too nice

he'd be a perfect friend
i hate myself for thinking that
but it's the truth
why isn't he my type
he's cute
he's sweet
too sweet

lot's in common
but only the nice bits
only the bits i let him see
he wouldn't like the rest

it would scare him
worry him
he'd pity me
try and fix me

i don't want that
i'd never want that

sorry sweet boy
you're better off with a sweet girl

x

maybe i'm bad

i lurk by the spotlight

one foot by light

the other by dark

i'll bask when i'm good

i'll hide when i'm not

x

compare me to the sun

i don't blame you for looking away

follow me long enough

and you will lose your sight

x

maybe i'm bad

i never see your face
but i've dreamt your lips touching mine
with hand pressed against my cheek

the thought of you
moves me   warms me

let my body burn
as i hear your footsteps
crush gravel as you near

take me from the wild
break me   make me yours

come out   come out   whomever you are
i'm waiting

X

i shout your name towards the sky
so that maybe you can hear me
not on fair days
when sky is clear of clouds
but on thunderous days
when storm fills every void

if we hear peals strike from heaven to earth
perhaps the obverse can be true
so when lightning strike
i shout
into a line that lasts but a heartbeat

strike again mighty zeus
i need to make a call
and make it a good one

i need my heart to reach above

x

maybe i'm bad

i find comfort at night

whilst the rest are asleep

every day i wait

for its shadows to hold me
wrapped safe again

x

stand the edge of precipice
and watch the world
as my life balances
in natures fickle hand
if this ground should fall beneath me
at least what i saw last
was a beautiful sight

x

technicolor rainbow
gleaming
across the wet tarred floor

how pretty
does the rain make the city
at night

x

strong dreams
focused too hard
can blind you
of your surrounds
making even small steps
seem impossible

with one trip
you will fall

but good trips
prompt strong holds
drawing cloud9
back to ground

clearing sight
for your true pursuits

x

maybe i'm bad

i got tired of waiting
for life to come

so i left

and dove into the deep

bare

hoping to find
new shores of new worlds

to grab and shake life itself
and shout

this is me!

but just in case i miss it
i've left behind a snare

x

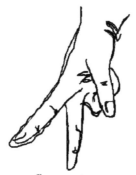

my fingers trace your scars

as i dance across your memories

x

maybe i'm bad

he fell for me that night
i saw it in his eyes

as we gently kissed
incessant flames flickered

they will dim in the future
but never die

it was decided that night
for my embers to
forever remain in baby blue

x

i will follow your footsteps
though your strides are long
you are my forever beacon
my guiding star ever strong

x

maybe i'm bad

he will be the one
who sees me in the dark

smelling of summer nights
of sweet grass and musky smoke

x

my dear petal

how delicate you are

so fragile yet beautiful

they say most pretty things are

shame they can't see those hidden thorns

x

my
face
without   a freckle
would be   like a
star   less
night   sky

i think we fall

to remind us
the strength of the ground
of which we callously stand

to remind us
our past pains we overcame
arrogantly now faded

to remind us
we are all but flesh and blood
we fall the same
bleed the same

fortune kicks all to the curb
and we must get back up
in need to go forward

so when i look down
to my scarred knees
i am reminded
these legs are strong

and if fate be willed
to challenge me again
i will cry out

come!
for here i will stand

X

maybe i'm bad

warrior princess

it's what my father always called me

do not describe me sweet
or he will bite

if you insist that i am
call me
smart
strong
unique
brave
first
and he will settle for a bark

x

my mother and i
have trouble seeing
eye to eye
but it doesn't
deter her love for me
nor mine

for my pocket
sized mom
has survived things
i will never experience
nor will she
with me

we have fought
separate wars
on separate lands
giving us
our separate views

we may see things
different now
but our hearts
will always stay true

for she is the warrior queen
who bore herself
me he and she
us fighters of three

x

maybe i'm bad

i dream the life i yearn
every day

sometimes

a lot of times

most times
i pretend i am living it
acting out scenes of my own desired play

the writer
the scientist
the adventurer

i read my script
i rehearse my role
i play my favorite act

as me

the girl who *lives*

x

do not fret
these dark waters
contain luminous creatures
who will show you the depths
of silent beauty

x

storm winds blow crooked signs
in this desolate town
guiding tourists
to roam backways forward
to white tipped fields
that stop rubber wheels

these signs'll get you lost

will say the old local
with blood roots deeper
than signpost steel
and forehead lined
like city maps
built not solely from
experience of others
but laid out plans
of own faults and gains

wandering'll get you your ways

he will preach

go seek what you can't see

x

the expectations
i have for myself
are far beyond that
which you had for me
they leave but a shadow
in my path of dreams

x

downers

how do i survive this

i think as i
dig myself deeper into this hole

no

not a hole
not digging

like quicksand

like i am stuck
in quicksand

and i am alone
trying to swim

trying to keep myself from sinking
but the more i move
the faster the ground
slips away

solid turned liquid
sucking me into the deep
swallowing me whole

x

with heart that pounds
i try to sleep

to close eyes
and imagine
something nice

but i can't hold
back the bad

anxiety fuels stress
my heart then burns

everything burns

why is it so hot
it's dead of winter

heart again pounds
to dream
of sweet release

just wanting
peaceful sleep

x

so shiny and round
perfect shade of red
with a slight pink hue

i look real sweet
don't i

you'll pick me up to see if it's true

you'll buy me
they always do

until you take that first big bite
you'll taste bitter instead of sweet

thus you'll toss me away
like the bad apple that i am

x

maybe i'm bad

i want so much from this life
it scares me

knowing i will never be satisfied

that it will be my hunger

which devours me
from inside

x

i feel
anxious
when
standing
in lines

i get
seasick

wavering
between
strangers

x

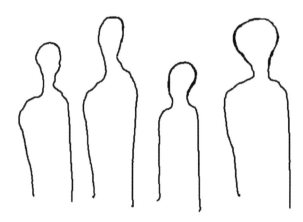

i keep my emotions
like pressed flowers
kept elsewhere
to have them lifeless and dried
until framed pretty between
two sheets of glass
dazzling for all to see
but none to touch
i'll give them away too
my lilies and daisies
of my insides now out

x

i'll have whatever everyone's smoking

this magic grass that grows from lawns
encircled by white picket fences
bringing banal bliss

i'll have whatever it is
to get me on board

i'll huff
and i'll puff

and i'll spin

        spin

                spin

x

maybe i'm bad

do you ever let worry
twist your dreams at night

leaving with you the impression
that near lurks a stranger

in a dark that fails to fade
even with open eyes

x

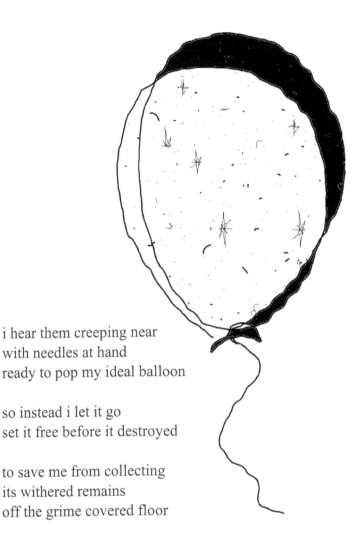

i hear them creeping near
with needles at hand
ready to pop my ideal balloon

so instead i let it go
set it free before it destroyed

to save me from collecting
its withered remains
off the grime covered floor

X

maybe i'm bad

what is in store for me
i wonder
i see those who have all
and all who get none

do i deserve more than either?
that is what bothers me most

not that i want it all so much
but so does everyone else

x

we are but fragments
collected through own journeys

building ourselves

piece by piece
day by day
year by year

and once complete
this puzzle mine
will fall back apart

year by year
day by day
piece by piece

i will slowly unravel
until the day
i lay
deep-six

x

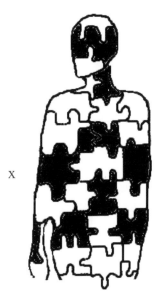

maybe i'm bad

close my eyes and tears will fall

for i will see your face

x

i wish
but am afraid
to step out of
this deaden calm

for what is peace
if not the one eye
of the storm

x

maybe i'm bad

every night

                                    i say goodnight

every night

                                    i say i love you

i have done so since
the day you entered
and the day you left

i say good night
i say i love you

                    my equivalent of a good nights prayer

i don't know if you can hear me
and i probably never will
but i will tell you nonetheless
every night

                                        always

                            that is my love

                        x

my mind muddled
day now night
night now day
i chase time past
and ruin what is gained

x

maybe i'm bad

each small problem
dropping soft like
snowflakes

i avoid and let them grow
grow
grow

an alps covered
in six feet snow

until that ill-fated
day when it comes

the roaring avalanche
knocking at my door

ending with me
buried
breathless

lost in cold depth

X

amie james

will you give me a push

when fear takes my legs

x

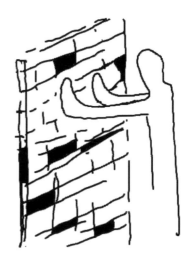

maybe i'm bad

my secrets   lay deep

           little by little they grow and keep

this mound   rises more and more

            until i feel it under my throat

i struggle to think of a way

           to keep this mountain at bay

but if this rooted mount be rid

         what will replace that empty space?

x

uncertain ills torment us most
wrote seneca

is that true?

knowing how most dreams end
and how others proceed

whether for good or bad
i feel kind of sad

uncertainty gives me purpose
to search for what is certain

to dive into the unknown
is to have hope

what a rush
what a life

truth be told seneca
it is the certain ills that torment me most

x

maybe i'm bad

it's hard to yield when
i know what's ahead

yet it's impossible when
i do

if it's good
i'll want to race towards it

if it's bad
i'll want to ram it down

x

i'm not good with relationships
but i like being alone

it's what i know
it's what i'm good at

like an inevitability
that i've grown used to
becoming scientific fact
that cannot be disputed

the moon has its stars
and the sun sets alone

x

to die or to live in vain
the latter is what she fears

now opting to risk her life
so that she may live

x

he made me pyramids of chocolate
and all i gave was sand

x

maybe i'm bad

she fails to understand me
and i have grown afraid to share
for her book has torn pages
tossed into the fire long before me
while mine are kept locked close

i will reveal only bits
until the time is right
for she will think everything
as me astray

what keeps me afloat
this growing drift
is our favorite flower
that will remain the same

my one thought of hope

is *we will always have
us a lily*

X

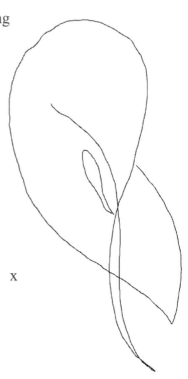

he pushed me asleep
when i wanted wide awake

x

maybe i'm bad

with each failing thought
that twists my heart
i tighten my fists

nails dig deep
to remind me with pain

this rage is for me

these grips
i hold tight

for loosened hands
show ill marked palms

i have an image to keep

us strong's are meant to be scrappy

not sappy

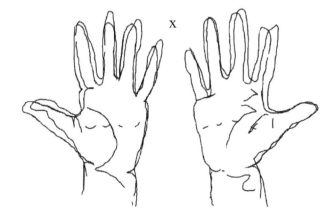

sometimes i want
to be hit hard
to snap me out
of my mind
into the here and now

x

maybe i'm bad

i tap out
after
the euphoric first stage
of love and like
before fantasy breaks
to show its defined face

X

they told me to
conquer the world
but never taught me how

x

she shouts muffled cries
not for rage
nor sorrow

but to tear herself
free from
societally caged breaths

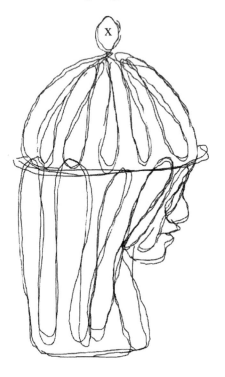

i hear your words
i see your smile

they are both very nice

there you stand so tall and bright
i move to evade your growing shade

those twinkled eyes and pearly whites
bring out in me not envy
but indication

your good-natured self
i feel in me is all
an act

beware your lies that drip off sharpened teeth
for i am no red hooded innocent girl

x

maybe i'm bad

these outsiders who lie on our streets
ones bred by our town
and don our collective filth

i pity them
yet lack the courage and strength
to lower myself
so that i may lend a helping hand

x

what well has the depth
to quench this thirst

ignore it long
and my mind may drought

x

placebo

i keep myself busy
to quiet my thoughts

x

maybe i'm bad

with the feelings i get

the pen that speaks the loudest

x

i want in you
the golden mean
of fantasy and reality

x

maybe i'm bad

i like secrets

so don't tell me yours

if i know too much

it'll break your allure

x

i've thought about becoming an escort

but then i'd have to take better
care of myself
for the sake of others

so that's never happening

x

i blinked and missed that shooting star
        and now gaze each night with wider eyes

x

i'll end up the old woman with the rusted gun
shooting at distant strangers
to watch them scatter and run

x

maybe i'm bad

be gentle as you go

or i may fall for you

x

amie james

i approach people
based on a
wavering streetlight

x

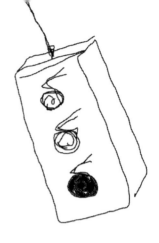

she laid on
the side banks
of burnt
yellow leaves
praying
for good karma

x

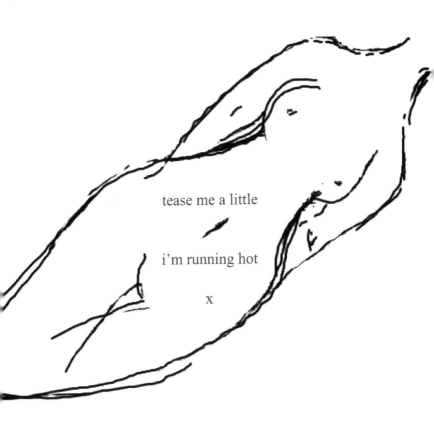

tease me a little

i'm running hot

x

maybe i'm bad

my soulmate
out there
beware
i will ask you to do crazy things
like to join me as i walk through fire

x

i saw you walking past

you were in such a rush
you tipped over

your gold rimmed cup

and you didn't even stop
to pick it back up

x

maybe i'm bad

i want the in-between
of the life that was
and the life that wasn't

x

of course i'll snap
when cornered

all animals do

and i am
a bitch after all

x

maybe i'm bad

close
my eyes
to follow the lights
that dance in my dark

focus on one

warp speed
into the abyss

flying falcon
on hyper drive through space

a one-person coaster ride
free of charge

to end with
dizzied open eyes

x

if you plan on
stabbing me in the back

make sure to
pull out the knife

if not

i will survive this
and come for you soon

not from the behind
i am not so little

i will come and face you
to see me run across your face

so be careful how you wield that knife

and never judge me
little

x

maybe i'm bad

cou cou!

am i crazy?

or am i french?

x

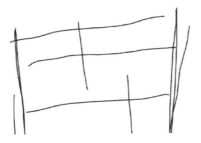

bitch and moan all you want
but try and keep it to yourself
it's all you ever do

wasting oxygen

and we are short on trees as it is

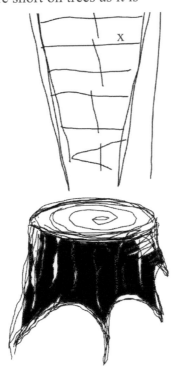

maybe i'm bad

you want me to care?
then make it worth my while

but for now when i see you fall
i can't help but smile

x

flare headlights at the rain
while sat in muted dark

and let idled hours weigh my thoughts
as sequin silver rushes around me

x

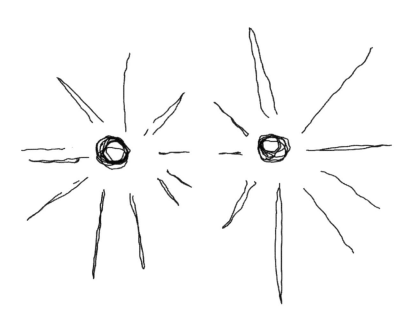

maybe i'm bad

i am most poetic
when i am tired and down

x

i breath
in and out

to try and keep
wondering thoughts

but with one word
one strain

they seep back in
this vernacular train

x

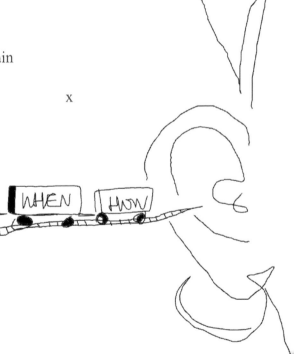

maybe i'm bad

will you be my vice
i miss craved intensity

the surge of body-fire
spreading from touch to touch

x

i saw you enter
and all went silent still

like first snowfall

x

maybe i'm bad

her fragrance is
gunpowder and roses

x

a sheep may see a lion in the mirror

until it meets one in the wild

x

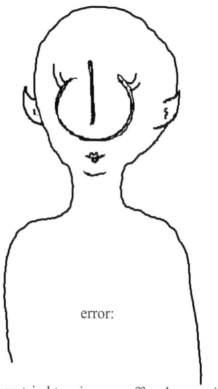

error:

have you tried turning me off and on again?

x

buzzing neon signs
gathering insects and
booze-soaked teens
seeking midnight delights

x

maybe i'm bad

hey you!

will you be the one?
to untie this perpetual knot

the one that sits in my gut
tugging at my heart

will you be the one?
the arthur to my gordian knot

x

dangerous things

live freely in

dangerous places

x

my melody can be a chaotic one

x

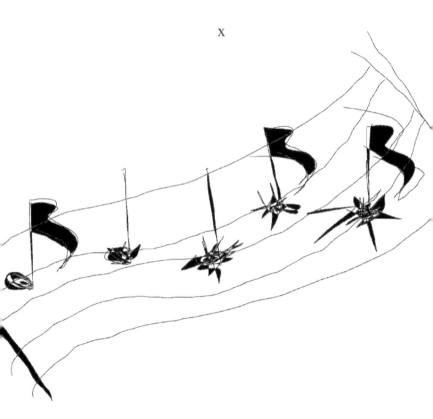

you think my voice some cry for help?

i never cry
rarely whine
this

is merely a breather

so

let me breath

x

like some of the contents
of this book

sometimes the things you
write
draw
or create
just aren't that great

i'll accept the fact that
maybe i'm bad
and choose to own it

to never let the fear of
being bad
stop me from being me

and neither should you

x

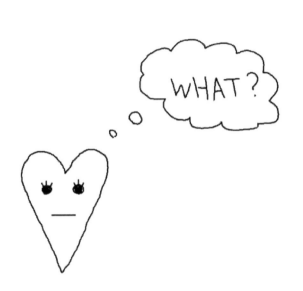

Printed in Great Britain
by Amazon